The Undying Faith Book 2. A Guide to a Life of Success and Happiness

The Undying Faith, Volume 2

Hebert McQuinn

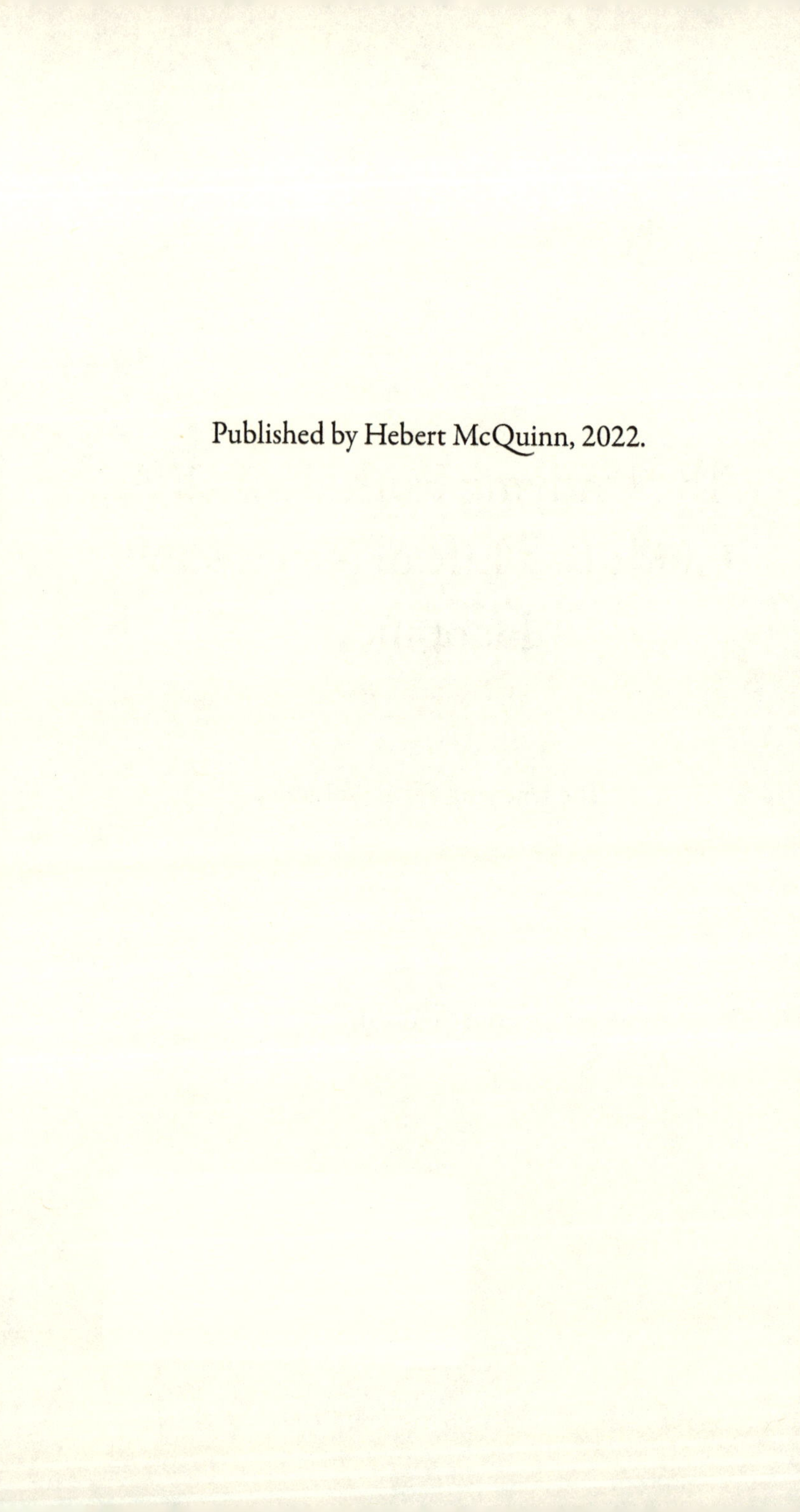

Published by Hebert McQuinn, 2022.

While every precaution has been taken in the preparation of this book, the publisher assumes no responsibility for errors or omissions, or for damages resulting from the use of the information contained herein.

THE UNDYING FAITH BOOK 2. A GUIDE TO A LIFE OF SUCCESS AND HAPPINESS

First edition. July 19, 2022.

Copyright © 2022 Hebert McQuinn.

ISBN: 979-8201160258

Written by Hebert McQuinn.

Table of Contents

Chapter 1

God and man: The connection

Genesis 1:26 says: "*And God said, Let us make man in our image, after our likeness: and let him have dominion over the fish of the sea and over the fowl of the air, over the cattle and over the earth and over every creeping thing that creepeth upon the earth. {1:27} So God created man in His own image, in the image of God He created him; male and female created He them.*

Genesis 2:7 says:: " *And the Lord formed man of the dust of the ground, breathed into his nostrils the breath of life; and man became a living soul .*" That is what the Bible tells us about the beginning of the relationship between man and his Creator. He made him in His own image and gave him dominion over all the other things He has created. The Concise Oxford Dictionary definition of a soul is, among other things " the spiritual or immaterial part of a human being, often regarded as immortal. " When God had finished forming man of the dust of the ground, he was still only just an object formed from the dust of the ground. And then we are told He breathed into his nostrils the *breath of life.* After that act of God, the creature was no longer just an object formed of the dust of the ground, we are told that he became a living soul.

From that point onwards, man became a spiritual being with something in him that is immortal. God has no beginning and no ending. There is nothing in God that is not immortal. He breathed His immortal breath into the nostrils of man so that it would be a part of him that will never die. What is immortal breathed immortality into the mortal and an everlasting communion thus began. This breath of life is the Spirit of God in man spoken of in 1 Corinthians 3:16 where the apostle Paul says: *"Know ye not that ye are the temple of God, and that the Spirit of God dwelleth in you? {3:17} If any man defile the temple of God, him shall God destroy; for the temple of God is holy, which temple ye are."*

That is the extent of God's proximity to man. He is not even nearer than near because saying that He is near implies distance between the two. He is not at close proximity to man. He dwells within him and is an inextricable part of him. It is clear from the foregoing that it was God's intention to be an inseparable from this special creature of His.

We have to bear in mind that the Bible tells us that He gave man dominion over all things in His creation, so the reason He wanted a part of Him to dwell in man was to effect and ensure this dominion. Man would have been unable to exercise the dominion if he had been created on the same plane as the other creatures and not connected to the power of the Omnipotent, Omniscient and Omnipresent God.

Breathing the *breath of life* into his nostrils was a very deliberate act to ensure that man's dominion over all things becomes a reality. This breath of life would be the Godly part in man that would enable him to establish his dominion over all things he had been put in charge of. That is how God delegated, in a manner of speaking, a portion of His power to man to make him a creative, thinking being capable of managing His creation.

When man became a living soul he became able to think. He became capable of thought, and we all know that thought is a mental activity. What this means is that from that point onwards he had a mind with which to think. Now thought is not something that can be seen because it is immaterial and spiritual. Its spiritual nature gives it its creative power.

The foregoing sums up how man got to be the creative being he is. Man's power to create came about in this manner, with God the Omniscient creator forming an alliance with this creature of His so it can be a creator too. When man creates, he knowingly or unknowingly taps into this immortal, creative power that is inside of him.

Now man has this duality about him that he uses in his creative nature. He has a conscious mind and a Subconscious mind. The brain is the seat of the conscious mind and the solar plexus is the seat of the Subconscious mind. There is an interplay that happens between the two minds when man is in the creative mode.

Man first conceives an idea with his conscious mind, which idea he contemplates to the extent that it appeals to and fascinates him. If it be something that he desires and wishes to manifest, in other words something he desires to have or to be, he will contemplate it and imagine what it would be like to have or to be that which he contemplates.

Now imagination is the mind's eye through which man is able to see things other than through his physical eyes.

Imagination evokes feelings normally commensurate with the physical seeing of whatever it is that is being imagined. When these feelings get to be sufficiently intense, they make an impression on the Subconscious, and the Subconscious, being the God force in humans, will immediately go about setting in motion all the forces that need to be mobilized to make all the resources necessary for objectification of the desired thing available through means incomprehensible to man.

Isaiah 55:8-9 reads thus:"*For my thoughts are not my thoughts, neither are your ways my ways, saith the Lord {55:9} For as the heavens are higher than the earth, so are my ways higher than your ways, and my thoughts than your thoughts.*" When the Subconscious mind starts to move all that needs to be moved for your desire to be realized it does so in ways known only to God.

We are as incapable of comprehending the how part of this process as we are incapable of comprehending how certain the organs of our bodies perform their functions without our awareness or conscious intervention, or how these same organs continue to function properly even while we sleep. There is a mind that directs the functions of the liver, heart, lungs, intestines etc without you even being aware of their activities and it directs them to perfection. This part of the human mind is the God force in humans. It is God's breath of life that we usually refer to as the Subconscious mind.

The foregoing shows how man combines with God to be a creative force so that the dominion he was given over all things can be realized. What makes man different from other creatures is his ability to formulate loftier ideals that serve purposes way above and beyond mere survival.

For instance man lived and survived many years on earth without electricity, but because he was equipped with a mind the extent of inquisitiveness of which enables him to think deeply and broadly about things concerning more than just survival, it was only a matter of time before he discovered this mighty force with which he transformed the world into a mini paradise, and through the use of which he has firmly established his dominion over all things.

I'm saying these things to bring home to the reader the nature and extent of the power inherent in every human being and the manner of its realization by his/her mere recognition thereof. As humans we have the power to do and be whatever we want to do and be because of this God force that is in us as the temple of God.

Part of the reason He dwells within us is to make available to us this stupendous power to create whatever we want to create and to achieve whatever feat we may desire to achieve in life. And we are only happy and successful when we are able to achieve what we desire to achieve in our lives. As it is written in Luke 1:37: "For *with God nothing shall be impossible.*" So you see that success is something that we're naturally wired for and not some abstract concept available only to a select few. Our belief in God makes everything possible for us. Through this belief we are able to manifest whatever it is that we may desire to be manifested.

Our God is the holy trinity of the Father, the Son and the Holy Spirit, and the Bible in Genesis 1:2 tells us that in the beginning when God created heaven and earth "the *Spirit of God moved upon the face of the waters.*" The Spirit of God is ageless, before the beginning, it was, and after the end when everything has passed away, it will be. Now this is the same Spirit that Paul talks about in 1Corinthians 3:16 and says that it dwells in us. It is that same ageless, immortal Spirit of God that was there before the world was, that dwells within us. It is my firm belief that at this point, the reader is able to appreciate the nature and extent of the power inherent in him/her to do and become whatever he/she may want to do and become. There is simply no limitation to that.

In Psalms 8:5 David says: "For *thou hast made him a little lower than the angels, and hast crowned him with glory and honour.*" Now, angels are heavenly beings, and man was made a *little lower* than them though he be a mere earthling. That is just how high we rank in the hierarchy of heaven.

On earth everything is beneath and below us. We are all powerful because we have the eternal Spirit of God in us and we know and believe that "with God nothing shall be impossible." If nothing is impossible with God and God is within us, vicariously there'll be nothing impossible for us also.

The Bible says in John 1:12: "*But as many as received him, to them he gave the power to become the sons of God, even to them that believe on his name.*" Now "sons" here is used as a generic term that includes both or all genders. To be a child of God implies that God is your father. And God has everything because everything was created by Him. Everything belongs to Him and you as His child are an heir/heiress to His vast estate which consists of everything there is in the universe. What is it then, that you could possibly ask of your Heavenly Father and be denied it for the reason of His lack of it?

In Matthew 7:7-12 the great teacher Jesus tells us: "*Ask, and it shall be given you; seek, and ye shall find; knock and it shall be opened unto you. {7:8} For everyone that asketh receiveth; and*

*he that seeks findeth; and to him that knocketh it shall be opened.
{7:9} For what man is there of you, whom if his son ask for bread,
will he give him a stone? {7:10} Or if he ask a fish, will he give him
a serpent? {7:11} If ye then, being evil, know how to give good gifts
unto your children, how much more shall your Father which is in
heaven give good things to them that ask him?"*

Now Jesus knew when he uttered these words, the nature of
the relationship God has with human beings and how He cares
about each and every one of us. There's no qualification that it
shall be given if you ask this way, or only this or that can be given,
or knock this way and it shall be opened unto you, no. All you
have to do is ask and all you need to do is knock, there is no
special way to ask or knock.

I doubt if there is a child who can doubt if it would be
opened unto him/her when he/she knocks on the door at his/
her home. With such an attitude we should knock also, not for a
moment doubting that it shall be opened to us, for the universe
is our home and everything in it is ours.

Everything is available. If you want whatever, just ask.
Anything that you seek you shall find by the employ of the
principle expounded above regarding the processes of the
Subconscious mind. Ask in prayer for whatever it is that you
desire to have or become and you shall have or become it.

1 John 4:12: *"No man hath seen God at any time. If we love
one another, God dwelleth in us, and His love is perfected in us.
{4:13} Hereby we know that we dwelleth in Him, and He in
us, because He hath given us His Spirit."* I shall pause here as
I consider the spirit of what I'm trying to communicate to be
sufficiently captured in these two verses. And it is simply the
reality of the interconnectedness of God and man that I seek

to bring home to the reader. He breathed the breath of life into man's nostrils so that He can dwell in him and likewise, that man can dwell in Him. Such is the nature and extent of the interconnectedness and interdependence between God and man.

This is the combination that has been and continues to be responsible for the creation and recreation of phenomena in the universe. By mutual cooperation with God, man, knowingly or unknowingly, has been able to leave the cave and its ways to enter into civilizations hat have saved him from an extremely difficult existence.

It is through the use of this combination with his Creator that man has moved from complete darkness into the dazzling light he basks in today. The underlying principle in creation and recreation of phenomena in the world remains this, that the conscious mind suggests ideas and the Subconscious mind organizes and produces what is required to give the ideas flesh.

Dear reader, please do not be concerned by the seeming qualification in the verses above, the casual reading of witch may give the impression that God's dwelling in us is conditional upon us loving each other, that this love for each other is a precondition for Him to dwell in us and us in Him. The reality is His Spirit dwells in every man. It lies latent in every man. It is only awakened and gets active in man when man recognizes it thus: Hebrews 11:6: *"But without faith it is impossible to please Him; for he that cometh to God **must believe that He is,** and that He is the rewarder of them that diligently seek Him."*

The precondition is the belief in His existence, he who would walk with Him must first and foremost believe that He exists and secondly believe that He rewards them that seek Him diligently. Diligence in this context I understand to mean careful and persistent effort. Recognition of the Spirit in us awakens and vitalizes it.

The belief that He is, permits His Spirit to awaken from its latent condition inside of you. The belief doesn't invite the Spirit from the outside, it awakens it in the inner man. And then we know that He dwells in us and that we dwell in Him because He hath given us His Spirit. I will deal with this all-important subject of belief in a separate chapter which I've dedicated to it.

It is one thing to have power. It is another to have power and know that you have the power. The value of power is in its utility. Otherwise it is just a latent thing with no value to the possessor. Unutilized, it remains mere potential, latent energy. It is however possible to utilize power if you possess it even when you are unaware of such possession, but the exercise of it in this case would be as coincidental as it is accidental.

But for one who is aware of his/her possession of power it can be utilized consciously and deliberately towards a particular, specific end according to his/her purpose. So a person who possesses power and is aware of such possession has a definite advantage over one who possesses it but is unaware of his/her possession of it. So it is with the power of God in you also, it value is in its utility.

God is in you and you are in Him. He is the Creator of all there is and as His child you are an heir to His vast, humongous estate. And Jesus our teacher says ask, and it shall be given you. He is not specific in terms of the things that you are allowed to ask because there is no limitation to the estate to which you are heir, it has everything one could ever ask for, and more. When you ask, we are assured, you will be given exactly what you have asked for. You will not be given stone when you have asked for bread, or snake when you've asked for fish. Whatever you ask, your wish is His command.

In Proverbs 23:7 we read that: "*As he thinketh in his heart, so is he.*" What you constantly think about, what is always uppermost in your mind, what dominates your mind, is what is in your heart and it's what you are asking for and you get given exactly that. As you **think** in your heart, so you are. That's the manner of our asking of the Lord, by the Law of attraction and that is why we have to be careful what thoughts we allow to occupy our minds for the better part of our time. You are what you feed your mind. If you constantly and continually feed it misery, you are asking God for misery, and it shall be given unto you exactly as you would have asked, and misery will be manifest in your life.

In Philippians 4:8 Paul gives us advice on a good mental diet: "*Finally, brethren, whatsoever thing are true, whatsoever things are honest, whatsoever things are just, whatsoever things are pure, whatsoever things are lovely, whatsoever things are of good report, if there be any virtue, if there be any praise, **think on these things.**"*

If you constantly think of such things and they are constantly in your heart, that is what you are asking for and you will be given exactly that, things that are pure and lovely. Paul knew the principle by which the conscious mind interacts with the Subconscious mind for the realization of the thinker's desires. The conscious mind suggests ideas and the Subconscious organizes the resources required to produce the ideas in the flesh.

In Matthew 6:33 Jesus tells us: "*But seek ye first the kingdom of God, and His righteousness, and all these things shall be added unto you.* " In Luke 17:21 he tells us: "*Neither shall they say, Lo here! Or lo there! For behold, the kingdom of God is within you.* "The first verse presents us with a puzzle, we are to seek first the kingdom of God and His righteousness for all things that we need to be self-sufficient and content to be added unto us.

In Matthew 7:7 He said he who seeks shall find. So when he says that we should seek the kingdom of God he knows that if we do that diligently we shall find the Kingdom. Diligence in the seeking is the only requirement and precondition, so it is not like there's any complicated stuff that we need to do to find the Kingdom of God.

The reward for the seeker is not in proportion to the effort put into the seeking at all, it is far in excess of it, which should be incentive enough for us to begin the search for this magnificent Kingdom in. And then in Luke 17:21 he hands us the missing piece of the puzzle on a platter, he tells us where to look for the kingdom of God, he tells us that it is to be found within us.

For we are His temple. He is the God that dwells in us. That is the nature and extent of the power inherent in every human being. We have the power within us and it is up to us to exercise it for our and the world's benefit. There is nothing we cannot succeed in because we have all power in us to do so. Since we have the Omnipotent within us we are all powerful beings.

God's Spirit in us is ever available and eager to grant us the desires of our hearts. We need only ask. I will talk about the how part of praying in a later chapter. For now it is sufficient to know that we have His **breath of life** in us. That we are in Him and He is in us and with Him, nothing is impossible. As it is written in Luke 1:37: *"For with God, nothing shall be impossible."*

He chose to partner with us from the beginning of time, much has been achieved with this partnership and much still remains to be achieved. All we need do is to exercise our power consciously and deliberately and direct it towards the attainment of our purpose, whatever it may be. To be able to do this, we must believe that He exists and that He is the rewarder of them that diligently seek Him. We don't have to be doing all manner of complicated and tricky things and jumping through hoops, we are told by the great teacher Jesus that all we need do is ask. It's as simple as that.

Now, we all have dreams and aspirations. Some of us are able to realize theirs and some aren't so able. Of those that do make the realization of their dreams and aspirations a reality, there are those who do so by sheer luck of coincidence, by fluke so to speak, and there are those that do so by conscious adherence to the psychological prescripts as expounded in this chapter.

The former group would need luck to be able to repeat the feat of making whatever dream come true because they are not following a certain, defined path but win by the haphazard method of hit or miss. The latter group however, can repeat whatever feat as many times as they need to, with much ease because it would be to them like following a definite formula, they just can't go wrong.

That is the advantage that people who are aware of their possession of power have over those who accidentally exercise a power their possession of which they are not aware of.

All of the above, to me spell only one thing, and that is, success can be made to order, the Biblical way. Unless you are a person who has pride issues, there's nothing easier than asking. More so if your receipt of what you are asking for is guaranteed. So it is clear that Jesus has given us a simple formula for success and happiness. We need only follow it.

Now the other thing I want to talk about is that in my life I have seen and known some individuals whose parents happen to be rich in worldly possessions, and I have noticed how the majority of these people are so self-assured and confident in their attitude towards life in general, with some of them, I must mention, being downright arrogant. Some are even disrespectful towards others because they happen to be heirs of these great estates, they have their parent's wealth behind them, and they get whatever they ask of their parents. They live lavish lifestyles of great opulence.

That is what a huge inheritance does to most children of wealthy people. But because all worldly wealth has a definite lifespan, in the long run that inheritance has no permanence. It is different from what you and I have. Our Heavenly Father owns everything, there's nothing that doesn't belong to Him, because He created everything there is in the universe, the wealthiest person's wealth is very, very minute and insignificant in comparison, in fact it is smaller than a speck of dust. We are heirs to the greatest estate of all, so by right we should be walking on air! When you take the foregoing into consideration, you will realize that our negative self-image and low self-esteem are totally misplaced.

Chapter 2
Transform yourself!

A man named Nicodemus, a ruler of Jews, once visited Jesus at night and Jesus told him that except a man be born again, he cannot enter into the kingdom of God. In John 3:4 : we read: "*Nicodemus saith unto him, how can a man be born when he is old? Can he enter a second time into his mother's womb, and be born?*" And Jesus answered in John 3:5 : "*Verily, verily, I say unto thee, except a man be born of water and of the Spirit, he cannot enter into the kingdom of God.*"

There are many Nicodemuses today who are still baffled by the statements of Jesus about the requirement for the second birth, and I must mention here that I find the coyness in Nicodemuse's tone a bit misplaced and indicative of unnecessary pomposity. But Jesus, being the wise teacher that he was, ignored the sarcasm and offered an explanation. That in itself is a lesson in humility. It's a lesson about suffering a fool without losing focus on what matters.

In the part about the need to be born of water Jesus was referring to baptism in a river as was practiced in those days and in the part about the need to be born of Spirit he was referring to the requirement that the individual believe in the existence of God and in the fact that He rewards those that seek Him with diligence, as a precondition for personal, spiritual transformation of that individual. Meeting those two requirements signifies the beginning of personal and spiritual growth that will lead you to finding the kingdom of God in you, so that going forward you will live in fear of nothing and in want for nothing.

Perhaps it may be proper here to delve into this matter of enormous significance, and it is that most people in many religions and denominations the world over, believe in a God is a being that lives in the sky, high in the heavens above. In other words they believe in a God that is outside of and apart from themselves, who needs to be invited and engaged in long and loud prayers.

I believe that from a Christian perspective, this state of affairs can be attributed in the main to the wrong interpretations of the contents the Bible by those whom churches charge with leadership of the flock of Jesus Christ. But, as the apostle Paul informed us in his apostil to the Corinthians, we, everyone of us is God's temple and He dwells in every one of us as individuals. He's nearer to you than near, He is nearer than the breath in your nostrils because He dwells inside of you and you and Him are one.

With that out of the way, we can go back to talking about the personal and spiritual transformation that one needs to undergo to be in a place wherein his communion with God can be firmly re-established. A lot of what needs to happen for the transformation to be realized is in the mind and how you use it generally, and how you must use it in order to gain knowledge that sets people free specifically.

Let us start by looking at where most people are that are who are living today. Let us look at the state from which they have to be transformed if they are to walk with the most High. This place is the space of the natural man. The natural man who relies solely on his five physical senses and his reason for knowledge of what is true and real or not, in his life. Anything that he cannot perceive with his senses and which his reason denies, to him does not exist or is simply not true. He is unable to believe in the truth of anything that he cannot see with his eyes, hear with ears, taste with his tongue, feel with his skin, or smell with his nose. For him the reality of a thing must be confirmed by its interaction with his physical senses, and if it's not thus confirmed, that is proof of its non-existence or its falsehood.

The apostle Paul in 2 Corinthians: 5:7 says: "*For we walk by faith, not by sight.*" This verse sums up the difference between the natural man and the spiritual man. Sight in this verse symbolizes the five physical senses. The natural man walks by sight because of his sole reliance on the physical senses for his knowledge while the spiritual man walks by faith because of his ability to perceive and experience things without the use of his physical senses.

For your transformation to be complete, you need to learn to walk by faith and stop walking by sight exclusively. This you must do by first establishing your communion with God by believing that He exists and that He rewards those that seek Him with diligence. That will awaken His Spirit in you for the workings of your partnership with Him to be possible. By your belief, that partnership is established and it is up to you to ascertain the terms and conditions for your benefit as a partner in the universe with your Creator, who has given you dominion over all of His creation. And those terms and conditions are contained in the Bible.

Jesus said you must be born again, of the water and of the Spirit. In Ephesians 4:22-24 we read: *"that ye put off concerning the former conversations the old man, which is corrupt according to the deceitful lusts {4:23}" And be renewed in* **the spirit of your mind** *{4:24} And that ye put on* **the new man.**, *which after God is created in righteousness and true holiness.."* After you establish your communion with God with your belief in His existence and His reward of those that seek Him with diligence, you have awaken the new man spoken of in the verses above. The 24th verse says that the new man is created after God in righteousness and true holiness.

It is you who creates the new man with your belief in the existence of God and His rewarding of those who seek Him diligently and thus acquire for yourself Godly righteousness and holiness. You die to the old man and his ways and you are born again when you put on the new man. Old things pass away and you become a new creature, or rather the old creature born again in different form.

You have a newness about you of a newborn and you didn't have to reenter your mother's womb for that to happen, as sarcastically suggested by Nicodemus when he spitefully touted Christ. When you have been renewed in the spirit of your mind and have put on the new man, the second birth is complete. It is finished.

Now, an electric kettle is still a kettle even when no eclectic current is flowing through it. You can fill it to the brim with water but nothing will happen to the water. So it is with the natural man. He has the make and capacity for righteousness and holiness but because he is not living in communion with God those attributes remain but mere potential energy, like the electric kettle filled with water but not connected to the source of electricity, it has the potential but currently not the ability to boil water. The moment you believe in God's existence and His rewards for those who diligently seek Him, you are connected to the source of power and things will begin to happen, like the kettle starts warming up and humming when connected to the source of electricity.

When a car is standing stationary and the engine is switched off, it cannot do what it was manufactured to do. It can't move. It is not alive to that ability. It is like the natural man, existing but not really alive. To make the car to come alive you have to turn the key in the ignition. Your personal transformation from natural man to man of faith is like that of a parked car whose key is turned in the ignition, the effect of the transformation is that you come alive. That is how to rise from death of the old man who is under the control of his senses and reason to the birth of the new man who walks by faith.

In order to be born again we must completely die to our old self so that the new self can be born. In other words we must completely abandon and leave behind the things and ways of the carnal man so that we can give the new man we're putting on full expression and manifestation.

Jesus warned us not to pour new wine into old wine skins. He advised us to pour new wine into new wine skins so that both can be preserved. Everything must be new. When you have renewed the spirit of your mind, your mind has new content and a new vitality. You are thinking different thoughts, thoughts of courage, hope and abundance. You are having a new mental diet and are for this reason, of good cheer for the better part of your time. When we habitually think the kind of thoughts that Paul advised us to think, we will be happier and more successful in whatever we endeavor to do. That is how we would be pouring new wine into new wine skins. We change our thoughts from those of fear, want and lack to those of courage, good health, success, happiness and abundance

Jesus in John 10:10 says: *"The thief cometh not, but for to steal, and to kill and to destroy; I am come that they might have life , and that they might have it more abundantly. "* The thief spoken of here is that state of mind called the Devil. He that shields you from knowledge of the truth that would set you free had you heard and heeded it, and whispers in your ear that all this stuff about walking by faith and not by sight is just hogwash. All this he does so that you may not share with Jesus in the inheritance of your Heavenly Father, and so that you may then die in your sins. That is how this thief kills those that he captures.

The natural man can sound real clever when he makes his argument against walking by faith, and he can make walking by faith seem like a real stupid idea. He thinks and reasons like that because the thief has stolen his ability to be conscious of his spirituality which would enable him to share in the inheritance of His Heavenly Father.

For as long as he considers spiritual things to be foolishness, he cannot discern them and thus loses out on the immense power that is available to the spiritual man, which he could otherwise leverage for his own benefit as he may wish, if he were to be born again. He is like an illiterate person who accuses those who can read of being fools. Absolutely absurd.

Jesus says he came that the natural man might *have life,* and that is because in his current state the carnal man breaths and walks but does not really live, and once he has touched him and has made him to have life, Jesus makes him to have it more abundantly than he could have ever have had it before he touched him. Our God is a God of abundance and in Him there is no shortage, no scarcity.

The spiritual man is able to experience life without the use of his physical senses. He is able to perceive things other than with his senses. When he prays and believes that he receives that which he is praying for, in line with the principle outlined in Matthew 21:22.

He can see the object of his desire clearly in his imagination and the feelings of possession and gratitude are to him real even though the desired thing cannot be perceived with the physical senses yet. He perceives it as a real thing in his inner world. He is the blind Isaac but he is not deceived by someone else, he deliberately deceives himself to give birthright to the younger son, the content of his imagination. He is Jacob crossing his hands to give the bigger blessing to Joseph's younger son instead of the older.

The notion of believing that you receive what you are praying for when you pray, before the possession thereof becomes an actual fact in the outside world, in order to ensure actual receipt at a later stage, is for the carnal man the height of folly. And yet this practice is based on a very sound psychological principle which many of the enlightened people of the world continue to this day to use to their advantage.

Paul's call is for us to be renewed in the spirit of our minds. We're called upon to change our mental attitude from one of want, need, lack and weakness to one of faith, hope, courage and abundance. Our mental attitude must be renewed, it must be made new because we have now put on the new man who has communion with God in righteousness and true holiness.

2 Corinthians 5:17: "*Therefore if any man be in Christ, he is a new creature; old things are passed away, behold, all things are become new.* "That is what happens when a person starts to believe, when he gets connected to the source of life, when the infinite power courses through the veins of the finite. All things become new when you have been renewed in the spirit of your mind.

In the discussion of personal transformation in the Bible, frequent reference is made to the mind because the mind is central to the success of the transformation. As you *think* in your heart, so you are. Never mind the association of thought with the heart in the verse. This was just a manner of speaking in biblical times, it was the linguistic style of those times. We all know that thinking is an activity carried on in the mind, whose organ is the brain.

The mind is the link between the finite and the infinite, between the mortal and the immortal, between God and man. It is the force that is to be used in connecting man to his Maker so he can cooperate with Him in manifesting His glory. It is through the use of his mind that man is able to do things successfully to the glory of God his Creator, who has from the beginning partnered with him for the purpose of the creating and recreating phenomena in the world. There was a decisive intent about God's breathing the breath of life into the nostrils of man. It was the sealing of a glorious partnership. God living in man, man living in God and the two being one as the result.

Ephesians 2:19-22 reads thus. *"Now therefore ye are no more strangers and foreigners, but fellow citizens with the saints, and of the* **household of God.** *And are built upon the foundation of the apostles, Jesus Christ himself being the chief corner stone. {2:21} in whom all the building fitly framed together groweth unto a holy temple in the Lord. {2:22} in whom ye are builded together* **for an habitation of God through the Spirit."** There it is. In black and white. You have been built for the habitation of God through His Spirit. That same undying Spirit that was there before the beginning of time, that will be there after time has elapsed. Human being, how great thou art!

It doesn't really matter how far gone you are in destitution or just how hopeless your situation may seem to be, you can be transformed into the person you dreamed of becoming before whatever disaster struck you. The biblical prodigal son, we are told, was at the point where he was eating swine food, food meant for consumption by the pigs in his care.

That was for him the turning point. He remembered how well his father's servants ate back at his home. And then he decided that he wasn't going to spend his life in regret and being too proud to humble himself and retrace his steps. Luke: *{15:18}* *"I will arise and go to my father, and I will say unto him, Father, I have sinned against heaven, and before thee, {25:19} And am no more worthy to be called thy son: make me as one of thy hired servants."*

Sometimes all it takes is a decision and a silent resolve to act on stemming the tide of destitution, to really find oneself. Remembering who you were before you experienced whatever misfortune that landed you in this negative environment, and working on a plan to return to the life you had before, one you can still have, is what you need to do. The boy's plan was to humble himself, wake up the following morning and go back home to his father and apologize to him. He would then ask him to make him as one of his hired servants. His plan worked like a charm.

His father was over the moon about his return and gave him expensive robes to wear, threw a huge banquet in his honour and they all had a big, happy celebration. The son never had to eat pig food anymore. That is exactly what happens with anyone who had gone astray and became estranged from his God. When you remember the opulence and luxury that you left behind when you were mislead by whatever influences, remember also that He is still your father and you are still His child and heir to His infinite inheritance. Awaken His Spirit in you and share again in His power, then do and be what you want to do and be.

Chapter 3
Confront and overcome your fears

Fear not. Do not fear. Do not be afraid. Those are the first words that would be uttered by God and His angels respectively when appearing before a human being and wanting to convey a message to him/her. It is not easy for us to follow, understand and comprehend what is being said when we are in the grip of fear.

In a frightened person's mind there's despair and panic. The object of his fear dominates his/her mind and he/she has less capacity for thought about anything else. A person who is in fear is unable to concentrate on anything else for any length of time. He/she can stare at the person talking to him and hear little or nothing. Fear causes its victim to be mixed up, distracted and unable to concentrate on anything.

That is why God, His angels and His son always first urged a person that they would to convey a message to, not to be afraid. They did not want to deliver the message to a person when the mental state in which he/she is, is such that he may not be inclined to have a full and clear comprehension of what is being said to him/her. One who is in the grip of fear is unable to listen attentively enough to be able to follow instructions well and without fault or error. Fear makes concentration difficult if not completely impossible depending on the degree to which the person is frightened.

I know that from personal experience because during my school years corporal punishment was lawful in my country. Parents and school teachers could lawfully use physical violence to discipline their children or children who are in their care. The belief prevailing then was the ever famous one that says if you spare the rod you spoil the child. Perhaps that was true to some extent and subject to some qualification but I won't get into that for the purpose of the message I want to convey in this chapter.

Now, the thing is that over here as elsewhere in the world, this power to met out corporal punishment was often used wrongly, in the sense that it was not only used to enforce discipline but also to force school children to learn the subject taught by the teacher who beats them up by force as it were. Children would be beaten for getting the answers wrong or for not understanding whatever aspect of the subject matter that the angry teacher is responsible for teaching them.

In primary school I did not learn much of the things I needed to learn in preparation for high school because hey, they beat us up almost daily. I lived in real and constant terror of my teachers. In high school I was doing math and science, among other subjects and both my teachers for the two subjects were two of the worst sadists I have known in my childhood.

From the time they entered the classroom to the time they left, my mind would simply freeze and fail to take in anything they had to say. I would be continually tense in their presence and I would be too eager to keep up with the class leaders, but the tension would get in the way of my understanding whatever was being discussed. I just couldn't relax enough to hear and understand anything that was being said clearly enough for it to make sense.

As a result of the fear I had of my teachers I learnt very little in the classroom. I only got to have a glimpse of what math and science were really about when I eventually formed a study group and learned the subjects from my fellow students in a calm and relaxed atmosphere where there was no risk of me getting beaten up by anyone.

The knowledge that I gained from that study group in four weeks far surpassed the knowledge I have gathered in twelve years of schooling. It is the most difficult thing to follow instructions when you are tense and terrified. The heavenly Beings knew the effect of fear on a person's ability to concentrate. That is why they would first try to reassure and calm a person down before they convey their message to him/her.

Now the other thing about me is I grew up a sports person. Soccer was my life. When I was not at school I was at training and practice sessions with my teammates. Over weekends I would be involved in official fixture games for my team. At practice I was simply the best player on the field. I was a constant best performer but I cannot for the life of me, remember an official game where I performed to at least half my potential. Official games were a periodical nightmare I couldn't wait to wake up from each time.

My good form at training didn't carry over to the official game environment because of fear. Before the game I would put myself under pressure with those nasty "What if" questions. What if I fail to mark my opponent and he went on to score that winning goal against us? What if I were to perform badly and cause my team the game? What if the spectators would laugh at me when I make a mistake? That was the other thing, I was too afraid to make a mistake in a game.

Bottom line is I had a wrong attitude towards my game that caused me to be tense and fearful going into the match and I became a completely different player from the one that is always on song at practice sessions. There I was relaxed because the stakes were not high, there were no spectators or opposing team. It was just me, my teammates and the coach. I thoroughly enjoyed myself in this environment hence I always put up man of the match performances because there was no fear and tension in me. I was in the right frame of mind at training and practice sessions.

Now adopting the right frame of mind is important in whatever that you want to do. Elimination of tension and a focus of all your attention on nothing but the task at hand is what you have to do to overcome fear. I don't know if it is possible or advisable even, to be completely fearless, but I know that there is a way to make fear disappear, like the morning mist. To eliminate fear like light eliminates darkness, you just remember that with God, who is in you, nothing is impossible. Take your attention away from the fear and focus it on the task at hand and the fear will take care of itself.

I remember when I was studying law at the University of South Africa, I have had to deal with fear of failure during each exam period. I would often wake up with butterflies in my stomach on the morning of the day of the exam, I would be jittery, worried and question whether I had done enough in my preparations to ace the exam paper that day.

Then I would recognize Mr. Fear's antics and quickly check myself. I would get out of bed and consciously take in the morning scenery outside, breathe in the fresh air, make breakfast with my attention completely withdrawn from the fear. I would then play my reggae records for inspiration and motivation. By the time I left home for the exam venue the voice of fear would be very tiny and small. It would have been reduced to a small tiny whisper. And once I had entered the exam room and was seated at my lucky desk, I would call on God's help and fear would from that point completely disappear.

What would have remained would be just a little of what people in the performing arts would call stage fright, which quickly disappeared once I had perused the exam paper for questions to which I knew the answers.

The other thing about God is He is able only to work with confident, courageous people. We saw Him preliminarily thrash out this matter with Moses before He sends him to the king of Egypt. He carefully worked on his self-confidence by encouraging and reassuring him.

He only gave him the first instruction when He was sure that he was in the right frame of mind, confident and courageous. In Joshua 1:9 God talks to Joshua: *"Have I not commanded thee? Be strong and of a good courage, be not afraid, neither be thou dismayed; for the Lord thy God is with thee whithersoever thou goest "* Thereafter Joshua was able to bark instructions to his troops bravely, with confidence and with authority, and he executed his military tasks with the necessary confidence.

If I were to cite every instance where God used similar words to deal with fear in someone and to give them courage to overcome their fears, I would make this chapter unnecessarily long. So I will only cite a few. In Deuteronomy 31:6 God said: *"Be strong and courageous, fear not, nor be afraid of them: for the Lord thy God, He is that doth go with thee; and he will not fail thee nor forsake thee. "*

God was preparing His people for battle and He knew how important it was that they be in the right frame of mind going into the battlefield. They had to be confident in their victory over their adversary when they set foot on the battlefield. And He intervened personally to ensure that they were free of fear.

Even in sporting events some sports people lose a contest not because they were not good enough to win or their skill set wasn't as top shelf as that of their opponents, but only because they feared them. They go into battle jittery and partially paralyzed with fear and the battle becomes much harder than it would have been had they gone into the arena relaxed and confident.

In Deuteronomy 31:23 we read: *"And he gave Joshua, the son of Nun a charge, and said Be strong and of good courage for thou shall bring the children of Israel into the land which I sware unto them; and I will be with thee. "* Whatever challenge it may be that you are faced with, don't let fear get the better of you. Pay no attention to it and just act in spite of it if you can't ignore it, and you will find that it disappears as soon as you have started to act on your plan. Fear likes attention, the longer you focus your attention on it the larger it grows and towers over you like a giant.

It is therefore important that we act with courage always because we know that God is on our side and with Him nothing is impossible. In 1John 4:4 we read: *"Ye are of God, little children and have overcome them, because greater is He that is in you, than the one that is in the world.* " He that is in the world are your problems, the challenges you face in your quest for success, the enemies that criticize you and try to trip you.

And He that is in you, He that is greater than the one who is in the world is your God, through His Spirit in you. I've heard it said once that we must stop telling God how big our problems are and instead tell our problems how great our God is if we are in need of courage to face them. I can't agree more with that sentiment.

The danger with entertaining fear excessively is that it has its sidekick called doubt, the archenemy of faith. When fear has disarmed you, he leaves you in the capable hands of doubt and he will make sure that your dream dies even before it is born. He makes sure, if you entertain him, that your desire never sees the light of day. In James 1:6-7 we read the following: *"But let him ask in faith, not wavering. For he that wavereth is like a wave of the sea driven with the wind and tossed. {1:7} For let not that man think he shall receive anything from the Lord.* "There it is, doubt revealed as the killer of faith and as the thing that drives a wedge between man and his Creator to destroy their partnership.

The Bible also shows us the power of doubt over one who entertains it in the story of two men walking on water one day. Peter and Jesus. Jesus bids Peter to come and join him in walking on the water of the sea. Peter jumps out of the boat and walks on the water towards Jesus. The wind gets strong and he takes his eyes off Jesus, who is the source of his power and looks down at the water at his feet and then starts to doubt the possibility and sustainability of this water walk stunt and as a result, immediately begins to sink into the sea. Jesus had to rescue and reprimand him thus *"Oh thou of little faith, wherefore didst thou doubt?"* His doubt killed his faith and made the continued walk on water unsustainable.

In Matthew 14: 27-31 we read: *"But straightaway Jesus spake unto them, saying, Be of good cheer, It is I, be not be afraid, {14:28} And Peter answered him and said, Lord if it be thou, bid me to come to thee on the water. {14:29} And he said, Come, and Peter was come down out of the ship, he walked on the water, to go to Jesus."* The above passage has been for a long time and is still to this day, very much a subject of controversy, and is usually cited when people challenge the veracity of Bible stories. But we will not get into that debate here.

What we see here is a demonstration of the power of faith when fear is not a factor. First Jesus warns the disciples not to be afraid when they see him walking on water and reassures them that it is him. Peter then walks on the water towards Jesus and all is hunky dory. Two men walking on water and not afraid because of their strong faith. The lesson in this story is that if you have enough faith and are not prone to fear, nothing is impossible to you. You can do anything you want to do anyhow you want to do it.

Further down in the same chapter, in verse 14:30 we read the following: *"But when he saw the wind boisterous, he was **afraid; and beginning to sink.;** he cried, saying, Lord, save me. {14:31} And immediately Jesus stretched forth his hand, and caught him and said unto him, O thou of little faith **wherefore didst thou doubt?."***

Now, let us analyze this passage. When Peter saw that the wind was getting boisterous, he became afraid, in other words he was overcome by fear. And immediately he began to sink, he couldn't continue the miracle of walking on water.

From what Jesus says to him when he saves him, it is clear that fear and doubt attacked his faith and rendered it powerless so it could not sustain his weight on the water anymore. We also learn from what he says to Peter that it is characteristic of people of little faith to doubt. And like I said somewhere in this chapter, once fear enters into a person, it tends to invite doubt so that together they can paralyze the person's faith in God and in him/herself.

This is a deadly combination if ever there was one, and the only safeguard against it is to never pay attention to fear in circumstances where it does not help you to be fearful, or to simply act in spite of it.

Then it cowers away and as it slowly disappears, confidence grows and when it is all done, a realization dawns that there was no need for fear to start with. So don't focus on fear too much.

Chapter 4

The magic of believing

Now finally we come to this all important topic and I hope to, in this chapter, give it the kind of analysis that it deserves. I'm saying this because belief is a concept that is foundational to practically all religions, not only Christianity. Jesus, on many occasions used to tell people that he had come so that those who believe in him should not die but have everlasting life. That is the extent of the importance of belief. If Christ is to be believed it is in this context the difference between mortality and immortality. It is the difference between the finite and the infinite.

In Hebrews 11:6 we read the following: "*But without faith it is impossible to please Him, for he that cometh to God **must believe that He is,** and that He is the rewarder of them that diligently seek Him.* " I take it that he that comes to God was not with Him before. He comes because he is seeking Him. But it is a precondition to finding Him that he must believe that God is, in other words that he exists. This principle is so fundamental and foundational to the very existence of the Christian religion in particular and religion in general. That is the nature and extent of the power of belief.

Belief is an essential part of faith. It is impossible to have and exercise faith without belief. You cannot have faith in God if you don't believe in Him. Likewise, it is not possible to have faith in any other thing or person if you do not believe in that thing or person.

Belief is as inseparable from faith as doubt is inseparable from fear. An analysis of the content of the above verse reveals that you cannot find and have God in your life if you don't first and foremost believe in His existence. This is absolutely imperative, because it is the principle that awakens the God force in you and vitalizes it.

Everything else in the relationship between God and man is dependent upon man's belief or lack of belief in God. And in the exercise of faith, if there is no belief nothing can happen according to that faith because it is devoid of the thing that gives it its essence, it is an empty kind of faith. Belief gives vitality to faith. Faith is a concept that is impossible to construct if belief is not first established. It is thus nonsensical for anyone to claim that they have faith in something or someone that they don't believe in. That is something that is simply inconceivable.

Everything begins with belief. I've heard countless times when a sports person is interviewed after winning a contest and he/she would say that he/she went in to compete and was not sure if they would win because their opponents were also good at the sport. They would then say that however, when they reached a certain stage in the tournament, a quarter final for instance, they started to believe that they can go all the way to win it.

So even when you are not absolutely certain about clearing the hurdles when you start out, you can eventually start believing during the proceedings, that victory is possible and that on its own would give you the impetus you need to catapult you to the heights you need to reach to win.

I have spent about six years of my working life as what in my country is called a shopsteward. Now a shopsteward is a trade union representative in the workplace. He/she must be conversant with the labor laws of the country and be conversant with the collective agreements concluded between the trade unions and the employer organizations as well as the organizational policies of the employer.

Now, the duties of a shopsteward include representing employees at disciplinary hearings, at conciliation and arbitration hearings. That is a huge responsibility that the shopsteward must shoulder in service of the union members as a trade union representative in the workplace.

Now, in representing an employee accused of misconduct, as his/her representative at his/her disciplinary hearing, the shopsteward could be the only entity standing between the employee and his/her possible dismissal from employment. At conciliations and arbitrations the stakes would invariably be just as high.

I would prepare for a case thoroughly before the date of the hearing. I would interview witnesses and prepare them for the hearing, and I would consult my sources of labor law. In short I would leave no stone unturned in my quest to ensure readiness on the day of the hearing.

Eventually that day would come and I would enter the venue of the hearing with the employee/s I would be representing in tow. When we would all be seated there would be this uneasy silence just before commencement of the proceedings because of the tension that would be in the room invariably. I would without fail be tense on the occasion, and at the back of my head would be fear of failure in the form of "what if" questions. I would be wondering how well prepared the employer representative is and what evidence they would adduce on the day and my imagination would run wild, making me tense and a little afraid.

I knew, even as these thoughts raced through my mind, that it would be fatal for my case for me to go into the proceedings gripped with fear, however slight it may be. So I had this routine to take my attention away from fear and it was that I would just out of the blue, when no one expected it, crack a joke and have everyone, including the employer representative laughing and looking at me like " hey, this guy!"

I would then have eased the tension and paved the way for the presiding officer to get the proceedings underway. At that point I'd have forgotten about fears and worries and doubts and I'd be poised for victory and nothing less. And everything that I would be saying and doing from that point onwards would be said and done in order to justify my belief that I'm winning the case. And nine out of ten times my belief would come through for me and I would win.

In Mark 11:23 we read the following: "*For verily I say unto you, That whosoever shall say unto this mountain, Be thou removed and be thou cast into the sea, **and shall not doubt in his heart, but shall believe** that those things which he saith shall come to pass, he shall have whatsoever he saith.*" Doubt is mentioned here again. I did say before that it is the enemy of faith and when it attacks faith it can render it paralyzed. You cannot have your mountain removed and cast into the sea if you have doubts about what you are saying, but if you believe that it shall be as you command, so shall it be.

Now, to clarify, the mountain spoken of here is not a physical mountain. No person can have that kind of faith. No person can possess faith strong enough to be listened to and heard by mountains. This is just a figure of speech in which your problems and challenges are likened to a mountain. The lesson in the passage is that however insurmountable your challenges may seem, belief without doubt is the key to overcoming them.

If you believe without doubt that you have it within yourself to overcome the challenges, you shall overcome them, one way or another. A word of advice, it is easy to muster the kind of belief that is completely devoid of doubt by remembering that He is greater that is in you than the one that is in the world. You are capable of overcoming your obstacles, if you only believe. The power to overcome is in your belief.

In Mark 5:36 we read the following: *"As soon as Jesus heard the word that was spoken, he saith unto the ruler of the synagogue,* **be not afraid, only believe.** " News had reached Jesus and the ruler of the synagogue that his daughter had already died. The people who brought the news beseeched him not to bother Jesus anymore because his daughter who was sick was now dead.

Jesus had every intention of raising that girl from the dead so people would witness the glory and might of God, but he knew that he wouldn't succeed in his quest if the father was afraid and did not believe that he, Jesus would solve his problem and raise his daughter from the dead.

The Bible says that when Jesus got to the man's house there was a noisy crowd that had gathered there. The Bible says that when Jesus got there he told them that the child was not dead but sleeping and he was going to raise her, we are told that the crowd began to laugh at and jeer him.

The Bible says that he took with him into the house only his disciples and the parents of the child and left the unbelieving crowd outside. For what he was about to do, he did not need the negative energy exuded by the unbelieving people to get in the way. He did manage to raise the child from the dead the Bible tells us. It is in this story also important to note Jesus's attitude to fear and belief. His statement to the child's father upon hearing the news of her passing indicates that he wanted him to remain positive and hopeful regardless. He wanted him to believe that everything was going to be alright.

The Bible also tells us that Jesus did not perform many miracles or heal many sick people by his normal standards when he visited his hometown. The people there did not believe that he was the Messiah sent by God. They believed him to be a charlatan because they knew Joseph and Mary and his brothers and sisters. That is how powerful the concept of belief is. In its absence even the Messiah was unable to perform at his best. It shows that the belief of the local people was behind the miracles and healings where he performed these plentifully.

In John 4:50 we read the following; "*Jesus saith unto him, Go thy way, thy son liveth. And the man **believed** the word that Jesus had spoken unto him, and went his way.* "The man to whom Jesus was speaking had come to him from a place far away and his son was sick to the point of death. Jesus did not go with him to see his son. He only saw the belief in the father and pronounced his son healed. Such is the miraculous power of belief. The Bible tells us that at the very time, to the minute, that Jesus pronounced him alive, the boy was healed. And it was because his father believed that Jesus was able to heal him without even getting anywhere near him.

Let me here share my story of personal triumph over a formidable adversity through belief which I call determined belief. Now I used to be a smoker of cigarettes, a heavy smoker, I must add. I started smoking during my high school days back in 1983. I had gotten to a point where I couldn't be without cigarettes on my person for one minute and I was smoking a pack of twenty cigarettes a day. That was when I wasn't stressed or under any kind of pressure, in which case I would easily smoke thirty cigarettes in a day. The more stress I found myself under, the more cigarettes I smoked. I was what was called back in the day a chain smoker.

Now, I was so addicted to nicotine that I couldn't go an hour without smoking any time I was awake. If a meeting I was attending would take longer than an hour, I would excuse myself for five minutes or so to go and have my nicotine fix, even when I was chairing the meeting or taking minutes. I had to ask someone to stand in for me while I went to perform my hourly ritual.

I used to smoke in bed before I sleep, otherwise sleep wouldn't come, and if I were to wake up in the night for whatever reason, I would immediately light up and smoke. When I woke up in the morning I would light up and smoke. If by any chance I would wake up in the night and finish my cigarettes, I would get out of bed, get out of my pajamas, dress up, leave the house, get into the garage, start the car, drive to the convenience store at the filling station that opens all night, buy a twenty pack, puff away, drive back home and back to bed.

After meals and after drinks it was impossible for me not to smoke. I was at a point where I did everything I used to do just so I can smoke afterwards. I was a nicotine slave by all accounts. Feeding the habit was also very expensive for me but I was afraid to even calculate the monthly cost of my addiction because it would depress me although I felt powerless to do anything about it. I had times when I would wake up in the night and cough so painfully. But immediately the coughing spell subsided I would reach out for my cigarette pack.

My situation was that hopeless. There were times when I would think about quitting the habit but it would only because I would be hurting and desperate. During such times it would be like I have nicotine sitting across the table from me and I would be trying to serve him with divorce papers so to speak. I would go like "Dear nicotine, I don't want to consume you anymore. I want to end our relationship once and for all and I don't want to have anything to do with you again, now or ever. " And nicotine would be looking at me coyly with his head tilted to one side, with a wry smile on his face: "Really now? Dear Hebert, that performance of yours deserves a standing ovation, very entertaining, but let me ask you a few questions hey. How are you going to go through one day without smoking? What are you going to do with yourself after meals and drinks? Do you think you will be able to fall sleep without smoking that last cigarette? "That would invariably settle it. The conversation would end there and then and I would sheepishly go and buy another pack.

Long story short, in April of 2020 during the first Corona virus lockdown in my country there was a ban on cigarette sales and it was a trying time for smokers countrywide. I was lucky because I had a friend of mine who ran a pub and had cigarette stock with him when the ban was imposed. I asked him to supply me with cigarette for the duration of the ban and he obliged. In the evening of the last Sunday of April the president of the Republic announced that the ban on the sale of nicotine products would be lifted on the last day of the month and all the smokers were very happy.

However our celebration was short-lived as the minister tasked with leading the health council established to issue regulations to combat the spread of the virus announced on Wednesday night that after considering the health risks for smokers during this time of the Corona pandemic, it was decided to prolong the ban on the sale of cigarettes indefinitely, until further notice.

Let me not bother you with the details of how that affected the smoking community. I, at this point decided to have another conversation with Mr. Nicotine. This time I said: "Nico my boy, I think I have what it takes to stop having you for my constant companion. Do you remember those times I was ill and hospitalized for a week or two? Aha! For the duration of my hospital stay I was not allowed to smoke and I was able to live perfectly well without you in my bloodstream. I would only resume smoking after discharge from hospital, after days of not smoking. That experience has proven to me that I can live and go for a long period of time without smoking. Now I intend to voluntarily impose this period of no smoking upon myself now and survive like I survived when I was hospitalized, and I'm going to impose it indefinitely because I think that you and I are done, for good. You just watch me " And I didn't listen for the reply.

I thought to myself I I could pull this off and that last day of April when I went to bed I had smoked what I told myself was my last cigarette. I had said my goodbye to my boy Nico. I honestly **believed** that we were through. That I only had to go through the first day without smoking and then take it one day at a time from there.

I woke up the morning of International Workers Day, May the 1st in the year 2020 a very determined man. I woke up and made myself a cup of coffee, sipped on it nice and slow, keeping my mind off cigarettes. At 10am I hadn't smoked yet. By my standards that was quite an achievement and I was greatly encouraged. My belief grew stronger by the hour and I went to bed that night without having smoked a single cigarette that day. I fell asleep and slept like a baby, and the rest, as they say, is history.

I had managed to beat four decades of addiction just like that. Because finally I believed that I could actually pull off that miracle. At the time I'm writing this I hadn't smoked a cigarette for 26 months. Glory be to God! I believed, and pulled off that miracle.

I had to write about that experience because I think it can actually help some addict out there who might be wishing to quit but not knowing how. Whatever it is that they may be addicted to, there is hope. They need only believe. Now let's go back to the scripture to learn what else it has to say about the power of belief. In Matthew 22:21-22 we read the following: *"And all things, whatsoever ye shall ask in prayer, **believing, ye shall receive.**"* My sentiments exactly. Nothing is impossible to him that believes. When you pray you must believe that you receive that which you are praying for and it shall be as you believe.

There was a time in my life when I considered myself to be down and out. I was in my late twenties, unemployed, destitute and only just having started to recover from a bout of depression. The future was practically bleak. I myself felt that I would be extremely lucky to find employment in the state I was in. But I didn't remain in that gloomy state of mind for long. Gradually when I was healing, I got to a point where I felt that I could dare to hope for a better life for myself. The more I thought about it the more I believed that I could make a grand comeback.

I felt at the time that if only I could get a couple of thousands for startup capital, I would be set for life and I wouldn't even need anyone to employ me anymore. I believed and hoped against hope that I could pull off this miracle and make something of myself regardless of the seemingly insurmountable challenges I was faced with at the time.

My belief, in that dire situation, resulted in me actually finding a temporary job that would set me up for bigger things than I thought possible for me when I started believing I had some kind of outside chance of making a comeback. I went on to obtain two diplomas in Road Traffic Management, the basic six month one and the advanced three year one. I went on to find me a job and worked for fifteen years as a Traffic Officer and a Peace Officer. I will write more extensively on my achievements in the autobiography I intend to write soon. I just mentioned the above to further illustrate the power of belief.

Chapter 5
Consciously deceive yourself

In Joel 3:10 we read the following: *"Beat your plowshares into swords, and your prunninghooks into spears: **let the weak say, I am strong.**"* In preparation for this war, an instruction is issued to the effect that the weak man must say that he is strong. If the self-deception were to be effective and actually work, the general would have an additional strong soldier where there was once a weak one. We have to daily make positive affirmations to the point where we actually believe that we are what we tell ourselves that we are, that we are strong, though in actual fact we be weak.

If you by any chance are going through a hard time right now, and things are just not going well for you, and maybe the whole world seems to be in a conspiracy against you, I wrote this chapter for you and others in similar circumstances.

I want to first make mentioned of a word that I would say is notoriously used to denote a situation where someone has been led to act to their own detriment. That word is mislead. I want to make constructive use of this word and say if your situation seems bleak and hopeless, and you feel that you don't stand a ghost of a chance to turn it around, now is the time to *mislead* yourself into believing that you are quite capable of overcoming the humongous challenges that are facing you right now.

Please do it and I tell you that you will be glad you did. Deliberately mislead yourself into believing that you have the capacity to fight your way out of this tight corner that life has pushed you into. Mislead yourself because that would be planting the seed of belief in yourself. Just tell yourself repeatedly that you can and eventually you will.

There are these words that motivational speakers, mentors and coaches tell people to utter daily, those words are called affirmations. You are supposed to say these words, hear yourself say them frequently and believe them, believe what you're saying to yourself about yourself and your capabilities. Speaking these positive affirmations out loud every day when you wake up, every chance you get in the day and before you go to sleep is a way to mislead yourself into believing the best about yourself and your situation.

In any situation you may find yourself in you are faced with a duality of options. You are the blind Isaac who must give your blessing to only one of your sons. And those sons of yours are the older, carnal or natural man who walks by sight only and the younger is spiritual man who walks by faith. Your blessing gives the right of birth to the son you bestow it upon. But unlike the biblical Isaac, you are not to be deceived by your son, you are to deceive yourself to give the birthright to your highest ideal. This you must do in spite of the protestations of your physical senses and your reason.

You must complete this self-deception by constantly holding the mental image of your ideal in your imagination as a fact that is already accomplished. If your reason tells you: "Impossible!"

Tell yourself "Possible!" many, many times, up to the point where the possibility assumes a credible naturalness to you. When your senses intervene and tell you that you are still in the same old familiar surroundings and neighborhood and your conditions remain unchanged, pay no attention to them and constantly meditate on your ideal state. Keep it alive in your imagination.

Any psychologist will tell you that we are as we see ourselves. Our self-image is the mental image of ourselves that we naturally live up to. As we think in our hearts, so we are. So it goes without saying that if we want to change who we are and transform ourselves, we have to change how we look at ourselves, we have to change how we perceive ourselves. To be able to achieve that we have to change our inner conversations, in other words, what we tell ourselves about ourselves, our conditions and circumstances. That is where positive affirmations come in if you are the kind that prefers to verbalize thoughts.

Optimal use can be made of this psychological principle by resort to the following exercise: Sit yourself in a comfortable chair in the house. When you feel that you are comfortably seated let go of your muscles, deliberately relax them one after another from the top of your head to the bottom of your feet to rid yourself of any tension so that you are in a state of complete relaxation. Completely immobilize your body and close your eyes.

Now there is this event that you know is certain to occur when you have realized your dream. Your family congratulating you on your promotion at work or on landing a job and they hugging you one after another, or you lifting the trophy after winning the tournament, whatever occurrence that is surely to follow the achievement of your goal, play it out in your imagination while your eyes are closed.

Let this scene play itself out over and over in your mind until you are oblivious of everything else around you. Hear the shouts of celebration from your family members and feel the hug of everyone, smell their perfume. Feel your teammates lifting you on their shoulders, hear their song and chant of victory. Hear yourself singing along. Make the scene as real as you can possibly make it to be. Play this scene over and over in your mind until it evokes feelings of joy and elation.

Or if that would be too much trouble for you, you can while seated there in a relaxed state induce upon yourself a state that is like sleeping, apply for sleep and while the application is pending but you are still only feeling drowsy, make your affirmation and it must be affirmations that signify that your desire has been fulfilled. You must express gratitude to a high power that made the fulfillment of your desire possible. Things like "Thank you, thank you thank you " or "isn't it amazing, isn't it just so very amazing?" "Isn't it juts fabulous?" Any sentence you may think of, words that you are accustomed to saying when you have received something wonderful. You are saying these affirmations in your mind as if you are saying them having realized the fulfillment of your desire. Repeat this exercise daily until it has a naturalness about it and the related feelings are more real.

Now the Subconscious mind can be deliberately controlled and directed by clever use of the conscious mind. Like I said previously in another book, the role of the conscious mind is to make suggestions to the Subconscious mind which suggestions the latter will act upon and set in motion all the forces that are necessary for the objectification of the contents of the suggestions. I have said previously that the Subconscious is the God force in man. The how part of its business should be no concern of yours because no man is capable of figuring it out. God did say after all that His ways and thoughts are as higher than our ways and thoughts as the heavens are higher than the earth. That is how you bless the younger son and give him the birthright.

In Ephesians 4:22-23 we read the following: "*That ye put off concerning the former conversations the old man, which is corrupt according to the deceitful lusts; And that ye put on the new man, which after God is created in righteousness and true holiness.* " Here is the duality that I talked about in the beginning of this chapter, the old man and the new man in the same person. I made the example of the blind Isaac and his two sons, the older and the younger one.

We are admonished to stop our former inner conversations and put on the new man. We must stop talking to ourselves the way we used to in the days of old, to stop those conversations with our former corrupt and lustful self and be born again to become the new man created to be like God in righteousness and true holiness. We must die to the old man by changing the way we look at ourselves and live according to our new perception of ourselves. Our inner conversations must change. We must learn to talk to ourselves in a new way.

We must deliberately mislead ourselves into being people living in a world of humongous possibilities, into believing that we can be and do anything we want to be and do. This step is imperative for the interaction of our two minds to take place in the context of positivity for the realization of our desires to happen.

The writers of the Bible were knowledgeable about many of the psychological principles that have in recent history gained universal acceptance. But according to the dynamics of the era that they lived in they had to clothe these principles in allegory and symbolism, which was according to the literary tastes of their audience at the time.

When you have put on the new man you are born again, old things are passed away and all things are become new. You are now a person with endless possibilities in your life. You as a new man are created to be like God in righteousness and true holiness. Your powers as a creative being are firmly established. You can do and be whatever you want to do or be.

To the natural man all the foregoing is just mumbo-jumbo. Pure hogwash. Because it is impossible for him to discern things of the Spirit. First he has to come to God believing that He exists, for the renewal to begin. But his problem is that he is unable to perceive Him with his physical senses and his reason also denies the existence of such a Being. So even the possibility of him ever coming to God is simply out of question. He dies in his sins.

In Mark 9:23 we read the following: *"Jesus said unto him, if thou canst believe, all things are possible to him that believeth. "* As with everything else, the technique explained above can bring you results only if you believe. When you believe, personal and spiritual transformations are possible with very little effort.

I did not have to apply a great deal of force or will power to quit smoking. I just decided and believed in the possibility of kicking the decades old habit. In fact thinking back I consider it one of the easiest things I've ever done in my life. All those years I was a prisoner to the habit I thought that quitting would be an impossible task, that kept me smoking and that false belief kept me from even trying to quit.

So successful self-deception is very, very possible. You can change your inner conversations and change your life. Your physical conditions, environment and circumstances must as a rule conform to and be in harmony with your perception of self. However hopeless your situation may seem, it only seems to be so and it is not necessarily so. Change your thoughts from those of defeat, poverty, lack and want to those of courage, hope and abundance and the character of your inner conversations will change. You will attract to you conditions and circumstances that are in harmony with your new perception of yourself. Let the weak say I am strong.

No one is condemned and imprisoned by his environment. You decide by your dominant thoughts and things you constantly whisper to yourself what your environment is going to be. By changing the content of your inner conversations you can outgrow your current environment and get out of it into one that is in harmony with who you have become on the inside of you. As within, so without.

The world that you see outside of you is a reflection of the world within you. There can never be any contradiction between the two worlds. You cannot see yourself in your own eyes as a poor person, habitually think thoughts of poverty, want and lack and be a rich person living in an affluent area in your town. That is an impossibility, an anomaly that is never going to happen even if you were to win millions in the lottery.

In Numbers 13:33 we read the following: "*And there we saw the giants, the sons of Anak, which come of the giants: and we were in our own sight as grasshoppers, and so we were in their sight.* "

This is the report of that the men Moses had sent to go and spy in the land they were to seize and occupy. The verse gives us an insight into how some people see their problems and challenges.

I mean, it's okay if the problems and challenges are humongous and all that, we all face those at some point in our lives. But to then see yourself as a grasshopper in comparison is something else. If in your own eyes you see yourself as a grasshopper, then your problem will tower over you as it would tower over a grasshopper and you will not stand a ghost of a chance to overcome it. The spies say that they saw themselves as grasshoppers in their own eyes, which maybe we can pardon as a delusion, but this thing doesn't stop there. They were as grasshoppers in the sight of their giants too.

The outside world reflects back to you what is in your inner world. If you see yourself as a grasshopper in your own eyes the world can't help but see you as a grasshopper too. If your inner conversations are those of a grasshopper, and that forms the perception you have of yourself, don't be surprised if in the sight of the world you are as a grasshoppers because that is how the universe works.

The way you treat yourself is exactly how the world will treat you. I've never in my life seen anyone being respectful to a hobbo and a tramp. Such a person sees himself as worthless and you can never be worth anything to anyone if you are not worth anything to yourself, if you are worthless in your own sight. That is the principle that is being expounded in the above verse.

The man who was confronted by a real giant on a battlefield was David. And he was at no stage of that confrontation as a grasshopper in his own sight. On the contrary he knew that greater was He that was in him than the giant that was in the world standing before him and shouting obscenities and insults. He saw in himself a man who was going to bring down this lousy giant with a huge thud. And that is what Goliath saw as he was falling from the impact of a stone thrown at him from a sling. He saw a very strong Israeli man. Deceive yourself.

Change the way you look at yourself If you want to change your world and your life. Mislead yourself into believing that you are the man sent to bring down the boastful giant that is your problem. Deceive yourself to believe that you are one of those who can make things happen for themselves. Master this technique and you can do and be anything you want to do and be. And it is so easy to master. Try it. You will be glad you did.

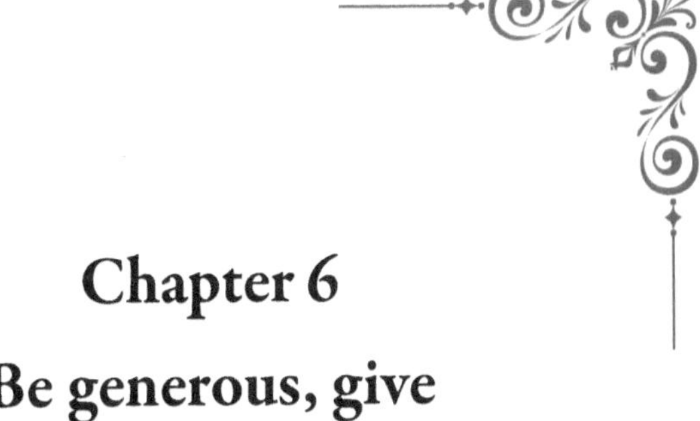

Chapter 6
Be generous, give

In 2Corinthians 9:6-7 we read the following: *"But this I say, He which soweth sparingly shall reap also sparingly.; and he which soweth bountifully shall reap also bountifully. Every man according to as he purposeth in his heart, so let him give; not grudgingly, or of necessity: for God loveth a cheerful giver. "*Giving is the sowing of the seed of a blessing. The act of giving is another way to bless the Lord and that is why He blesses the giver in return.

The size of the blessing that the giver receives is in direct proportion to the size of the gift he/she gave. It is a simple and straightforward arrangement, for a little gift you get a little blessing and for a huge gift you get a bountiful blessing. Now there is a requirement that the giver must meet for the gift to move God to give a blessing. And it is that the gift must not be given with misgivings or purely out of a sense of duty, that is, not grudgingly or out of necessity. I know that this requirement is quite a poser for many folks but it is what it is, don't give only because you think you must but also be cheerful going about it or your gift will not earn you any blessing.

How you purpose in your heart speaks to your motive in giving. You could be giving to alleviate a burdensome condition that the recipient of your gift is struggling under. Or you might give only to cheer up the person. You may also give for the joy of it. It doesn't really matter what the reason for your gift is as long as there is no evil intent and the gift is coming from a cheerful heart. There it is if you have been wondering exactly what is involved in the act of giving, it is an act of sowing the seed for a blessing.

In Proverbs 22:9 it is written: "*He that hath a bountiful eye shall be blessed; for he giveth of his bread to the poor.* "Now there is something in the verses quoted thus far that suggests that the gift must be sorely needed by the person to whom it is given. That is why the reason for the blessing of the person that has a bountiful eye is that he gives of his bread to the poor. Giving to people that cannot possibly repay you is the giving that is more pleasing to God. It is clear from a careful study of the scripture that the poor hold a special place in the heart of God and that He values and is more loving and kind to those who are loving and charitable to the poor and needy.

Besides it being the planting of the seed for a blessing, giving can also be a pleasing experience for the giver. Just seeing the eagerness with which the gift is received, the spark and glow in their eyes when they see that you are giving them something, the verbalizing of pure gratitude, for me makes me forget that there is more benefit to accrue from the simple act of opening one's hand to a needy one. Giving clearly has some spiritual rewards besides its being the sowing of a seed for a blessing. So if you want more, you should give more, then you will reap more bountifully. That is the simple, basic principle underpinning an attitude of generosity in general terms.

Now we all know that every person is different and unique in that no two persons are alike in all respects, and that there are some traits and characteristics that we seem to have been born with and that they seem to be written into our DNA, and that is so very true. Every one of us has inclinations and propensities, in other words, there is definitely conduct that we are more than likely to engage in because of the way we are in our character.

To some people generosity is like second nature, they give instinctively and that is just the way they are, or maybe they are people who have not known much lack and want so they have always had something to share, to me that is the likely scenario concerning this type of personality.

And I also happen to know that there are some of us to whom giving does not come that naturally, those who have to first interview themselves thoroughly before giving anything to anyone, poor and needy or not. I remembered that I once belonged in the latter category of people. I am still struggling with the whole idea that some people have made a vocation of begging, for instance. I seem to want to satisfy myself that this person is deserving of a gift from me, like the gift must be earned somehow, and that makes me meaner than I should be so I am working on changing all that

We do have, all of us, what psychologists call learned behavior. When a behavior is well learned and frequently practiced, there comes a time when it cannot be distinguished from behavior that is inherently natural to the person, to the point where it is practiced instinctively and automatically.

The point that I am making is we all can learn to be generous. We can all learn to be people who give instinctively and with a cheerful heart. All we need do to realize this is to believe that we can learn, and then practice this kind of giving as frequently as is possible. Even in this case I still believe that practice makes perfect. If we struggle much to do so we may pray to God for the ability.

In Proverbs 21:13 it is written: "*Whoso stoppeth his ears at the cries of the poor, he shall also cry himself, but shall not be heard. "* Okay, you have a discretion to give or not to give to the poor. No one is forced to do the giving. You are within your rights to just turn and walk away. But with that said, there are consequences in so doing which many are not aware of.

What you do to the poor gets done to you to the extent that you do it to them. When you give unto them it is given unto you too, and likewise if you refuse to hear their cries and refuse to show them mercy, your turn will come to be needy also and your cries will not be heard, they will fall on deaf ears. You will cry in vain. If ever there is any motivation to learn to be generous, this is it. It will make you successful and happy. Besides, when you come to think of it, your gift to that poor person could be the means he/she needs to reach his/her greatest breakthrough. So give I say. And it shall be given back to you many times over.

In Luke 6:38 we read the following: "*Give, and it shall be given unto you; good measure, pressed, and shaken together, and running over, shall men give into your bosom. For with the same measure that ye met withal it shall be measured to you again.*" Generosity is a Heavenly virtue that is greatly pleasing to God. It invariably moves Him to reciprocate and give favour materially to the giver in proportion to the size of his gift. God's measure cannot be compared with man's for His thoughts and ways are higher than man's thoughts and ways.